Poems from the Tom Fry

Jack Churchill

To Ellen
For the journey

[signature]

ISBN 978-1-365-83372-4

Designed by John Labovitz
Photographs by Michael O'Brien

Foreword

A quarter of a century ago I came to my new wilderness home on Tom Fry Creek in Oregon's Rogue River Country. As a retired political economist, I originally thought I was destined to write the definitive work on our nation's water policy.

That destiny came to an abrupt dead end half way through the outline process, when I stumbled over the poverty of the languages of the various disciplines that frame American water policy and turned to the language of Poetry.

I then began a long poem on the River (any and all rivers) to help me escape the stultifying boundaries of bureaucratic and academic writing. And I followed Williams Blake's guidance to generations of poets:

> I give you a golden string
> just wind it into a ball
> It will lead you in at Heaven's gate
> built in Jerusalem's wall

My long poem on the River became the starting point for a wide range of poetic inquiry into the flow of the river of my life. I employed a variety of poetic forms, from mini-ode to haiku. The poems here represent a collection from this rewarding endeavor.

Jack Churchill
April 2017
Agness, Oregon

Acknowledgements

I want to thank my friend Julie Norman for bringing this work to fruition and for typing and editing the manuscript. Jeremy Skinner's assistance in organizing the material was invaluable. Michael O'Brien provided the amazing work of his camera. I owe a deep debt of gratitude to John Labovitz of Uphill Art Farm for designing and publishing this book and providing his helpful encouragement.

I. Awakening

Streamwalking

It's over a hundred today
just perfect for streamwalking

Cast clothes aside the bank
merge into beckoning stream
water flows through my legs
I walk step after step
through lichen steeped canyons

Water sounds crescendo heights
cascades over silvery plumes
slides down chutes of bedrock
pummeled into flowing current
lounges deep in foamy pools
formed by eons of time

Leaves of alders and maples
ride canopy in wavering skeins
sun's light mixes flickering greens
twirl together in sky's blue

Rocks resounding earth's rhythm
sun's warmth radiating into soul
meditating deep in heavenly situation
joining ancients in spiritual reflection

It was really pleasant

Wondering

We are told to go and learn from the water
ROSH HASHANAH SONG BOOK

What is it about the river
or any and all rivers
that creates feelings full of majesty
for nature's sublimity

What is it about the river
or any and all rivers
that makes man finally acknowledge
power is more than human virtue

What is it about the river
or any and all rivers
that threads life veins
through nature's world

What is it about the river
or any and all rivers
that creates a special place
in a moment of time

What is it about the river
or any and all rivers
that have no beginnings
and never find endings

What is it about the river
or any and all rivers
that Native Americans
worshipped so heavenly

What is it about the river
or any and all rivers
that hosts the aquatic
and sustains the terrestrial

What is it about the river
or any and all rivers
that kindles my needle
to splice poetic threads

Running sands

This is where I come from
where the mountain meets the sea
where god E Kah Nie dwells
in sight of land sea and sky

Born amongst the tide pools
swirling in passing sands
life opens and closes
in reflection of sea anemone

Over sheep strewn meadows
where Nehalems left their footprint
I wandered in boyhood pursuits
nurtured in memories
of simple times long ago

I went to where I come from
with my son now grown
we felt the life we shared
but did not dam the sands
we felt the south wind and the rain
the sand between our toes

I looked beyond and saw
the passing of the times

Can I now?

Can I now sense the reality of the present
can I now breathe the breath without fear
feeling flow of universe in and love out
can I now hear the Tom Fry in all its pulses
singing and shouting its life's journey

Can I now feel breezes rustle trees around
and winds blowing horns of storm
can I now ride the surges of muddy Rogue
manipulated with engineering finesse
bearing the jet boats in shrieking caress

Can I now sense the pain of river Illinois
dealt by man's hands on watershed lands
can I now plant my roots deep
in the lands of the Tom Fry

Can I now hear Chief Seattle's wisdom
cry out Indian traditions
can I now feel in deep conviction
that white man's ways have soiled earth's condition

Can I now fear feel smell hear see love Nature's spirit
inhabiting every living thing in universal reality

How did you get there?

Beats me

It just seemed to happen
life unfolding day after day

So here we are today
adding 9 to my 0 or 0 to my 9
or as Lincoln dignified it
four score and 10
Or 101 if we count Oliver in

It has been bumpy
it has been exciting
living the American Century
14 presidents and one to go

Born under Mount Hood's shadow
baptized in Neahkahnie's ocean
I lifted my head off my pillow
to greet 33 thousand 2 hundred 84 dawns

From cranking phones and crystal sets
to internet and Apple watches
time moves
technology dictates

My stories have been many
my poetry conveys narration
seeks glimpses of Nature's wisdom
of people swimming in my life
of love of family and our times

Water has been my element
Father Sky and Mother Earth have sheltered me
Buddha and the Dharma have guided me
worlds of Nature's wonders have entombed me

Neahkahnie House

Stands on ocean front
under E-kah-nie's reign
sand sea and sky
capture Nature's elation

Built in gabled style
graying shingles cover
where five generations
walked their walk
and talked their talk

When the first train whistle
echoed down Nehalem's Valley
Arthur Churchill found
his Pacific home

Past Indian shell mounds
Little Creek tumbles by
singing tunes of
Nehalem's tribal gatherings

Mañana

They asked me what I did in Chacala
when I said I lived the word *mañana*
then smiled and turned their pro test ant minds
to things important
like work and recession

I came to know the pelicans
chased whales in wonderment
watched buzzards gathering
took siesta with intensity

I mused with hummingbirds
explored hibiscus beauty
eyes glazed on bougainvillea
dreamed of nothingness

I listened in the night
to breaking surf and silent sky
chickens crowed
dogs barked

I woke to streaking dawn
and wrote another poem

Table reflections

Oh yes
water has flowed
across this table
ten years and more

Age of the blue tooth
now crows our time
celebrating infirmity
in technology

Do we really know
how table conversation
has been circumscribed
by Gates, Jobs, and their ilk

We are morphed in miracle
of rapid flow
of words
of wireless and windows
of e-mail and internet
of messaging and imaging
of reincarnating
blueberries and apples

Has this somehow made better
our talk at table
our community understanding
or improved sacred beliefs and
ancient habits of being human?

Alas – here at Wolfe Street
even the door bell
has been transfixed
now in system format
with more yet to come

I harken thee here
let us listen to the table
and remember the simplicity
of the turkey and the stuffing

Fish on!
For Kass and Louise

George my Osprey neighbor
hovered in cohesive confusion
watching in circling diligence
as we humans slugged our beer
braised our burgers
talked our talk
sat on tailgates
loaded with fresh June snow

We gathered on this bar named 'squaw'
entitled by treaty of 18 and 56
to those of Indian blood
their rights to fish in all per pe tu ity

In this traditional and accustomed place
sand and rocks stride this stretch
where Rogue welcomes Illinois
fish poles dangle high-tech lures
snare dwindling spring chinooks

Here we of Agness gather
on a cloudy afternoon
to celebrate with twins of wrestling fame
their coming of age
and listen to the call of

    Fish On!

Again and again
history records on this sacred spot
the excitement of the splicing
the D N and A's
of woman and salmon

Two rivers

I spent a diligent Fathers Day in the garden
listening to the jet boats howl
skimming the Rogue in world class race

Seeing you at ten pulling mighty oar
catching the beat
in Deschutes River's harmony

It is you I think of
rowing down on Whitehorse
looking up at rimrock crests
flowing browns into blues

I see flapping wings of man's insolence
inject alcohol and fuel
into orifice of man and machine
striking rhythms of disharmony
foreign to Rogue's gentle calling

And now at twenty and four
rowing down on Whitehorse
sharing wisdom of your lore
to seekers of Nature's meaning
the father asks the son
how has the river changed you

Flowing together over time
river and you
you and river

Dancing sticks

I look out on jagged heads
barnacle-clad weathering grey
clinging mosses flowing green

Pilings mark these waters
where mills docks and canneries
once stood
and coastal craft and log booms
tied their lines

Can't you see them now
dancing jigs in tidal reach
as shades of soldiers
marching off to war

Like the trees that formed their lives
each casts its own shadow
on the running of the tide

Chinook

Chinook winds blow fair
shed winter's gloom
blood flows again
salmon seek their pilgrimage

My garden springs to life
weeds take the lead
I turn the earth
smelling spring

Snow

The snow paints a picture today
blending all of Nature's contrasts
into spectacles of quiet whiteness
a new silence calls forth
sharp and clean in winter's feel

Looking up

Into the Tom Fry I find my way
wandering in changing world
today was one of those times
when god's grace came to me

Alder canopies swaying high over head
sunlight filters through mottled skies
whispering leaves flutter so gently
weaving images of kaleidoscopic delight

Waters flowing down the creek
casting shadowy waves on rocky floor
as sunlight sparkles igniting rapids
in brilliant flashes of dazzling light

Wind whispering nurturing caresses
floating wisps of spring's gentle fragrance
water spirits dancing tunes in my ears
squirrel calling sharply for her mate

This spot I love and know so well
I sink into forest floor
feel the earth spin
my spirit floats into the sky

Coming home

The drums beat last night
sounding out cries of welcome
honoring runners carrying eagle staff
two hundred miles
all the way from Siletz

They carried the eagle banner high
bringing home symbols of the tribe
marched north in chains
crying tears of life
long ago

The ancestors raised their grateful spirits
seen dancing in the firelight
honoring youth carrying their staff
back home to Rogue River country

Moon and stars looked down
as drums beat on into the night
singing songs of tribal lore
carrying cadence to dancers
clad in buckskin and ribbon dresses
dancing special renditions
of meanings in native tradition

Did you hear as I did
way into morning's dawn
the drums of ancients
resounding in delight
from the freedom of their spirits
celebrating the circle of our life

II. Growth and Discovery

Awakening
Many waters
Spud Road
Dynamos
Whales I have known
Natalie's day
Cleaning house
Plane splash
Cavorting with Eleanor
It's a grape day
A Taurian sight
Fire
Intellectuals on parade
20 years of creative sweat
Citizen of the world
Farewell the boy
To my daughter Wendy
Oliver Zakai Churchill
Welcome Mei
It's Mei Day

Awakening

I welcome dawn this morning
and you, exotic red flower,
who came to beautiful fruition
during starlit night

Petals extend their bounty
waving your anthers
on bold erect stamens
hiding ovary in tender cover

Smells of jasmine and almonds
waft in morning stillness
teasing my senses
in endearing harmony

Open me in your glory
deep in feminine mystique
unfolding and encompassing
like sea anemone

Many waters

Where two rivers join
Shasta Costians called home
dwelling in Nature's harmony
sharing Mother Earth and Father Sky

Memories of time float from
this village called Tiegetlinten
savory smoke wafting
children's voices playing
braves hunting and fishing
women gathering nuts and berries
elders leading tribal ceremony
saluting mystery of salmon gods

And then miners and settlers
Billings, Blondells and Millers
planted orchards apples figs and grapes
farmed the land
roamed the forest
traveled trails hunting game
learned to read and use the rivers
and lived in isolated integrity

Today two-leggeds come again
to honor this ground rich in history
Patrick and Catherine site their cabin
newly built in pioneer tradition

Talon, Lexie, Shane and Gabriel
dream and play again
in freedom and Nature's wonder
sharing youthful memories
of the Rogue's deep rhythms
and the Illinois' clear blue call
where two rivers join again and again

Spud Road

There are not many roads
you drive every day
that seek adventure
every moment of the way

I can assure you well
the road we call spud
is one of those
that's not too sure
it's really a road

It's named after Spud
who grows tomatoes
when he and Jim
are not working
on the road

Its history is murky
I can tell you now
the old road slid down
when they cut the highway from below
and what we know as Spud
was temporary
or so they said

It's so steep you grit and grunt
grip tight
hold the wheel steady
and pray your rear
doesn't spin right out

Yesterday we got the grader
and smoothed all the bumps
first time ever
since Skinney's grader fell off the hill

So now we got a big bill
instead of a bad hill

Dynamos
a tribute to the Beat poets

Way up in the Cascades
poets shouted from lookouts
opened roads to Beat sixties
blew horns to modern reality

They gathered messages
felt winds
tapped sages
smoked dope
captured mountain spirit
sought Nature's secrets
tore flesh from icon symbols

Inward searching
scratching the Buddha
they sought truth
for our generation

Whales I have known

Once
many years ago
in a bay called La Paz
I met many whales

Spouts blowing
spray towering
whistles sounding
heads undulating
backs heaving
tails waving

Ten or more
huge Grays
moms and babes
danced their dance

In the Sound of Puget
Orcas roam the San Juans
all around Vashon
killer whales
show their colors
black and white
in joyous rhythm

Last evening in Chacala
they came close to shore
to meditate at Casa Jade

What fun to bask in surf
with setting sun
and frolicking whales

And today
Sandra and I set sail
in search of wondrous whales

Greeted we were
by spouting Grays
to the left and to the right

Transfixed in their action
I marveled long
on meeting again
wonders of the sea

Natalie's day

It's a naked kind of day
says Natalie
it's a naked kind of day
cause it is so hot

On the beach
east wind warms
white foam flies

Stream beckons
clothes shed
bottoms dip

Sands are dammed
time and again
Churchills prevail
til nature overcomes

Water flows
Natalie exalts
mud pies fly
in mindless glee

Collin jumps surf
springs in delight
shouts to challenge
wave after wave

Derek and Robert
converse in remembrance
dallying in boyhood bliss

Cleaning house

It feels good today
got the house all clean
from winter's dirt
and doggy smells
just need a visitor
to make things right

Clean up the mess
straighten out the bed

What is even better
is to sweep psyche clean
of the true clutter down below
erasing morass in mind and soul

Plane splash

Never a day goes by
here at Agness
when man and Nature fail to interlock
in some manner or another

Yesterday
was one of those days
an airplane fell
right off the runway

It seems the pilot
just came to fish

He parked his plane
cast his line
hooked his fish
heard the crash

Oh my gosh
        I forgot the chocks

And life goes on
at Agness International

Cavorting with Eleanor

If life's reality is
the awareness of the me
all else is really perception

I can assure you
sexual fantasy looms large
in thoughts I carry around

So enchanted was my libido
aroused in good humor
exposed to inviting desire
in words and gestures
that came to get me

Once again Eleanor
reaches far out
to dance maypole tunes
exuding sexual dialogue

Staged with twirling devilishness
motion and transition
regale sexual desire
flash orgiastic triumph

She opens forbidden fruit
looks to human reality
orifice language triumphs
we recount our sexual journeys
in memory and mind

She reminds us once again
there's nothing like a good fuck

It's a grape day

The vines are hanging heavy
with the makings of the wine

The weather has turned to fall
first rain drenched all

Empty five gallon buckets await
Betty Jerry Joan Jack and the dogs

Up and down the rows we clip
juicy bunches of purple grapes

Now the wagon is full
a hundred gallons or more

No bare feet on Stillwater Farm
just steam and technology

To get the purple stream running
to the juicer and barrels of good red wine

A Taurian sight

Lurking in the oven
rising to full height
browning mellow odors
wafting in morning light
it feels good
to know such delight

Fire

The day dawns still
fear seeps
which way the wind today?

Yesterday mushrooms billow
then explode bursting trees
into roaring inferno

Tonight guests come
oysters steak and fresh corn
our last supper?

Like in '48
when Columbia bellowed loud
we flee Nature's wrath

The Buddha says
'as it is'
impermanence prevails

       * * *

On a Tuesday morning
the air blows clear
what comes the day
where goes the fire

What to do
they say get ready
pack up your gear

And I wait

Moods swing
fire settles
quiet mornings
ominous afternoons

To defend or not
bulldoze my Nature
or let her rip

Go to town
get the u-haul
have lunch

With tears
salute the army
dozers and hotshots
advancing on Agness Road

* * *

What to pack
things
not much matters

It's my trees
my creek
me...nested in huckle brush

* * *

Loading out
Tim's muscles
get it done

On the other side
fire roaring
through forest crown
fed by gusting winds

Battalions of bulldozers
charging up and down

Twenty-seven miles
of Maginot macho
geared to fight mother

* * *

Air tankers vanish
to another fire?
we need political muscle
where's the pit bull?

* * *

Calm now
northwest wind blows
fire settles

Fire people come
I'm out naked
watering garden

Unabashed I say
good of you to come
wait til I get my pants

The verdict
house is indefensible
no escape route

Cut the brush
get more sprinklers
pray they say

Run like hell

* * *

Tim cuts brush
engines roar

Fire crews come
rake the yard clean

* * *

Dateline Agness
defending the western front
sixty more miles of fire line

On NPR
my neighbor John
reports from Agness

Neighbors feed reporter frenzy
down home wisdom blossoms
in New York and LA Times

3000 fighters move in
set sixty miles of fire line
crews from Canada

Mexicans in yellow
packs on their backs
Pulaskis at the ready

Dozers cut fire lines
helicopters backfire bombs
hotshots guard the fire break

Smoke fills the valley
helicopters scoop river water
damping the hot spots

West Florence Fire
moves ever closer

        * * *

What once was Florence
is now called Biscuit
alas
politics in fire too…

        * * *

Backfire planned
prepped and ready
sixty miles of line to hold

Hotshot Canadians Australians
New Zealanders and Mexicans
all stand ready
armed with torch and Pulaski

Helicopters armed with bombs
set the fire
stretch out their buckets and dump
retardant down the line

     * * *

Down on Lawson Creek
their backfire jumps the river
nearly burned my friends' houses

Roars up Nancy Creek
gobbles up ancient forest

Immediate evacuation ordered
drier than the desert
winds stand still
fire erupts

     * * *

The day dawns a northwester
more backfires lit
huge clouds of smoke
billow down the valley

Nature's fire
meets man's fire
whose side is god on?

Intellectuals on parade

I went to hear
what the Ologists
had to say

Biscuit Fire
what happened
how
where
why

hard metal folding chairs
heads facing front

serious people
one follows the other
armed with power point
threaded with graphs

hard core facts
isolated in functional slot
headlined in hypothesis
gorged in data display
triumphant in conclusion
forgetful in synthesis

no music
no poetry

20 years of creative sweat
a poem for the pioneers

What a year for those
who breathe co-housing
it's a millennium of sorts
a celebration of creativity
a place concocted

We heard the stories
we saw the pictures
shared the laughter
felt the anxieties

It's a tale of many parts
where man, place and Nature
set to work
co mingled in externality
to form a more perfect union

Is a commune a place
of bricks and mortar
or a flow of words
a crucible forging ideals
into practicalities?

Answers flow in the knowing
in the look and the feeling
of the milieu
cast in their ensemble

Citizen of the world

As you wander life's trails
in search of holy grail

We think of you here
in celebration of birth

We salute your spirit
in travels on our earth

We delight in your wander lust
and send thoughts of love and trust

Trek the passes high
follow clouds to the sky

Worship peaks of grandeur
probe high into yonder

Gird the steppes of Asia's vastness
seek peace in soul's fastness

Remember to hold steady
when crossing canyons heady

Sing your songs of bliss
as north wind whistles kisses

As breath of life flows
to and from your soul

Probe deep in universal secrets
sharing wisdom with the keepers

And when all goes crazy
just eat Jack's gravy

Farewell the boy

My boy has gone from home
strolling far out into the world
making the break into manhood
cutting last binders of boyhood

Waves of sadness flow through me
tears roll from rubbed eyes
joyfulness flows out of sadness
as each moment becomes reality

Passing through the rites
high school shaped the body
college stirred the mind
eastern travel flamed the spirit

Always touching Mother Earth
he sought the mountains high
calling on his father in the sky
seeking visions for life's journeys

To my daughter Wendy

I often bask in delight
that you and I
share this world

Brilliant eyes shine
smile lights your face
sending forth armfuls of love

Oliver and Mei are so lucky
to have such a mother
with such grace and tenderness
to share life's corridors

So as spring renews
and our garden greens
I reflect on the love
I hold in my heart for you

Oliver Zakai Churchill

We join in our spirits
alive in our awareness
in honor of the ancients
and in search for the beyond

We bow to the directions

From east flows energy eternal
south sends Nature's harmony
in the west oceans roll to moon's currents
out of north strong winds freshen clear sky

On this land of many waters
revered in Takilma tradition
we rejoice in ancient lore
to present to the world
and give name and presence
to our son Oliver Zakai Churchill

We give him our blessing today
and call upon the gods
for shield through future storms
and a life where waters flow clear

Your parents Wendy and Derek
bestow your name today
Oliver Zakai Churchill
in the waters of the Tom Fry

Welcome Mei

With a wiggle and a giggle
Mei flounces into tent
she brings love and smiles
swirling into family bosom

She springs from eastern heritage
spliced in ancient twine
packaged in modern China
in the year of the fire snake

The curtain opens
she walks onstage
arms in motion
feet a-waddling
lines well said
but not very clear

So now we see the family four
Oliver a-hugging
Wendy a-cuddling
and Derek a-smiling
all together now

It's Mei Day

Today we celebrate
closing arms around our Mei
cementing her in family world

Thankful for her spirit
so many vibrations
in rock-bound feet

The light she brings
in spunky strides
shakes us up
tries our senses

She sends her love
back and forth
in boisterous energy
and wondrous hugs

We all join in dotting i's
and crossing t's
adopting her in Yankee tradition
and clasp her to our family bosom

III. Passion

Comments from laureates

Beneath the veil of earth, sky, water
I hear the restless beating of the wings
RABINDRANATH TAGORE

Deep horns blast out
the coming of the
Earth – Tiger Year

We are gathered in the dawn
before Buddha's temple
awaiting
golden-hatted monks
escorting the Dalai Lama

In this crowd of Tibetans
aglow in dress of tradition

New prayer flags snap
out as rainbows
in Himalayan breeze

Overhead white clouds
move quietly
through mountain peaks

From the north come
ganders out of Siberia
a hundred or more
(they call them *Balaka*)

Beating leisurely wings
three times
they cir cum am bu late
before departing south
for Tamil Nadu

The message from the skies
subdues us
in silent whisper
as the drums sound
and horns shout

His Holiness comes
talks to us of peace
with-in and with-out
in humor and humility

A simple message:
'Today is ours
to do or not
as restless time
veils reality
and swings forth
into eternity'

Passing through Chicago

Landing in Chicago
engines of growth
growl through time
hub of history
web of fate
enchanted in elasticity

Hatching waves of promiscuous capitalism
feeding genes of masculine ego
jazz horns sound alarms in black rhythm
while careening freeways
carry screeching airplanes
through courses of airport obstacles

Hey Doc!

O'Gara is his name
still talks like Jersey folk

Has his practice
in a rambling house
set right on the sea
hunched under a big old tree

His dedication to human kind
is known world 'round

Hu mane ness
bubbles in his smile
glimmers in his eyes

He serves the young and old
from pre-natal
to post-thrombosis
he doctors all we got
or get

Honoring the past
he searches the future
to treat our ills
with more than usual skills

Diagnosis is his art
he blends
fine honed knowledge
with god given intuition

And we are most thankful
he is here to doctor us
today and every day
in our county of Curry

Guardian of public lands

On that day in 1905
when Pinchot and TR
carved out forests
on White House floor

On the 1st day they created the Forests
on the 2nd day they created the Forest Service
on the 3rd day they created the Forest Ranger
on the 4th day they created the Forest Supervisor
on the 5th day they created the Regional Office
on the 6th day they created the Chief Forester
on the 7th day all hell broke loose

What we have here today
is the Forest Ranger par excellence

Molded in his traditions
of forests, forestry, and publics
of forest plans and cut demands
of tree huggers and tree cutters
Mike has blazed his trail

Navigating the Chetco
enhancing the Rogue
Mike leaves his mark
on people and place

For in his way
with that gentle mix
of humor and dignity
he served the land
and people well

Thank you Mike
for living in your times
breasting waves of change
riding devolution's deathly grasp

A Ranger you have been
loyal to your tradition

A fighter in our forests

Well you're sixty now
past your prime and on the decline
checking into AARP and Medicare
and thinking on the easy chair

It's time to dredge memories
picture journeys traveled
smile on love's treasures

Your animal spirit I detect
a queen of the forest
roaming constantly seeing all
making opportunity reality

When stories are told
of forests and streams
Julie Norman stands tall

Led the charge
to save the land
repelled the predators
defended the ecology

She sings Nature's songs
as her camera records
the flowing of our rivers
the growing of the trees
and those who walked the lands

So celebrate the moment
meditate into the beyond
let the years just roll by
and share our love forever

Tiger in the Senate

Freedom rings today
as we stand in celebration
and honor the man
Wayne Lyman Morse

His voice heard loud
'round the land
carried clarion call
for freedom in our land

When those encased in power
stifled speech and freedom
hiding truth for actions expedient
Senator Morse sounded his trumpet

Defender of the Constitution
he warned time and again
to guard well our procedural rights

The essence of our being
is in the process
not the substance
of what we seek

In this troubled time
when again our government
seeks to stifle freedom
in the name of terrorism

Let us dedicate well his truth
in our dialogue in democracy

Copper Salmon
dedication of the Copper Salmon Wilderness

Long in history
will we sing
for those stalwarts
who joined in battle
to save this place
and river wild

Let us forget not
this land once foredoomed
marked in Congressional stone
cemented for annual cut

A-slumber in Bunyan's shadow
a band of stalwarts rose
they began a journey
long and tortuous
like Gandhi's march on the salt
a journey no Hobbit could endure

Their clarion call
for water's integrity
became a milestone
in preservation's fight

Let the record show
they predated Franklin's forest legacy
Clinton's Forest Plan
and coining of riparian systems

Jim and Jerry quiet in their manner
stealthy in their striving
gathered friends to the Elk
preached salmon's needs

Enemies they encountered
Ford, Hatfield, and South Coast
logger's inertia and myth
allowable cuts and fortress O&C
district rangers and forest supervisors
all strongholds of officialdom

Sounding their call
educating publics
building alliances
pounding marble floors
they made their case
gathered their strength
year after year

Today we pause
relish in their win
thank the troops
praise political actors
who brought this bacon home

But as Kennedy charged
'Let this day mark this time
when we go forward'
to protect our wild rivers
from headwall to estuary
to restore our salmon
in memorial right

Let us now give salmon
standing in this society
long accorded
to Native American culture

And in our fight for conservation
let this chapter
sing loud the tales
of Jim and Jerry
who stood
to save their place
in this our universe

Virgins at the altar no more

My friends Amy and Scott
trekked through Nepal
carved their names
on Tiger Rising movie
with pictorial pageant
imbedded in cultural story

The tale begins and ends
in the bowels of the village
hanging high on hillside vista
encircled in Nepal's wondrous beauty

Their camera portrays
the gripping iron of poverty
transcending rural peoples
all across our world

Courage-inspiration-acceptance-fate
march through time
as family saga
knits its way through the film

Hope and hopelessness
balanced in Buddha equation
tragedy and fate rise and fall
in Facebook characterization
of people and beasts

Scaling Everest-size peak
Amy and Scott
sign the summit book
descend with their story
totally wrapped in magnificent emotion

Advent of demise
we opened Savage Rapids Dam

No truer words were uttered
about a river
not intended
when Jean-Jacques Rousseau proclaimed
'man is born free
but is everywhere in chains'

Harnessing rivers
an affliction of mankind
a way to get them into the GNP
a manifest in engineer ego

Unharness a river
un-christen a dam
a truly unique event
in annals of river's fate

Let this day be remembered
as a milepost
in conservation history
where rivers gain standing
where precedent moves momentum

Fifty years ago...nineteen and fifty nine
I witnessed another celebration
we closed the Dalles Dam
yes we harnessed the Columbia
and waved 'So long to Celilo'

Today...two thousand and nine
freeing river of man's chains
is manifesto for many

We cut the ribbon
opened the dam
returned our Rogue
to flow in freedom evermore

Changing landscape
Florida revisited

Land shelled white
kleenex boxes with porches
form oceans of architecture

Phalanxes of high-rises
stamp our gator paths
as wind whispers in palms

Flag-toted undulating greens
center man's attention
imprisoned
in yuppie tradition

Architectural boredom
called Wind Song and Shell Point
Sea Scape and Gulf Cove
endow gated communities

Ribbons of spaghetti
spew traffic
east west north and south

Drums beat
tunes of tourist traffic
white beaches rumble

Native rivers of grass
retch in white man's
rivers of crass

Tele phallic symbols
guard endangered species
relocated in refugee camps

Formed like a still life
museums of Nature
remind our children of life
before freeways and TVs

People to infinity

In requiem we sing today
songs of life long ago

We sing to those
who walked this land

We sing in beat to drums
of years gone by

We sing our heritage
of this place

We sing to where we once belonged
and knew plant and animal

We sing to women grinding the corn
dreaming salmon's run

We sing to the people
vanished from their place

We sing to trails traveled
visions formed from mystery

We sing to deep canyons
tumbling sparkling waters

We sing to the salmon
creator and sustainer of life

We sing to coyote
enabler of myths and visions

We sing to our wisdom keeper
and all our wisdom keepers

We sing to new memory
of salmon ceremony

We sing our prayers for the people
reaching to infinity

Salmon quest

Gods and salmon merge today
in celebration of phenomena
known in ancient lore
today in paradigm

Totality of universe
comes into breath
as water flows
in circular motion

Ancient peoples nurtured
spirit and body intertwined

Sperm egg and DNA
cycle through the spectrum

Where the creek rushes
women in station
chant salmon connection

Listening
water drumming
hands molding
petroglyphs speaking
fertility is alive

Feather lady

As the rivers flow
rising on Siskiyou ridges
cascading down ravines
rushing through valley floor
flowing into western sun

Life and river run their course
always changing
each replenished
from sky above

Aggie cool in her wisdom
downloaded from generations
as heart guides her mind
through currents of the past

We stand together under Table Rock
she hears history's whisper
connecting shades of salmon
in archetype song

It was then
it is now
I stand in awe
of Aggie's beckoning feather
which leads me deep
with salmon's spirit

Salute to the crown jewel
dedicating Lake Oswego's North Overlook

As I look out from lofty pinnacle
on this day beginning my seventieth
I have a poem to share from wisdom
in vision for our commemoration

Truth is in this land
we celebrate today
ceded to the white
by Native Americans

They walked softly
on this common ground
sharing all of Nature's
flora and fauna

This sacred ground stands
where braves' vision
found reality in themselves
and the great beyond

As we reflect today
on the course we took
to save this open space
in our urban place

May we thank the vision
of citizen comprehensive planners
and all those just citizens
and public servants too
who fought the fight for public use

And forgive the greed and shame
both citizens private and public
who sought to fence
this land in private rights

Look out
look out in wonder
you and you
just plain citizens

See the view carved by god
of urban lake unrivaled
in all the USA

It has been saved
just for you
and more than
seven generations beyond

Guard this land with care
it is full of Nature's treasures
most fragile under man's hand

We can count the deer and herons
rare birds trees and shrubs
hardly found in other urban place

It's the crown jewel you now have
guard its fragile nature well
my citizens

For it will take constant vigil
that's the truth that will always be
in this land

Orwell revisited

Mountains of words pour
from White House speakers
all ending in war war war

Orwellian fantasies
now fashion
third millennium reality

Where are sons of founders
speaking liberty
and justice for all?

Leaders hunkered
under Senate desks
breathing fear and speaking naught

Tom Paine is dead

Henry Adams revisited

Is this a new encounter
American eagle vs Russian bear
transcending historic paths
                    or
Roman Legions rolling tanks
and CocaCola rewinding tunes
to Pax Americana
                    or
born-again Christian crusaders
embattling Moslem hoards
re-mobilizing Bible vs Koran
                    or
just the new world
staking crown
to all the universe?

New hands on deck

I feel more comfortable
with my hands on the reins
WINSTON CHURCHILL,
THIRD MEMOIR

The world breathes anew
history turns a page
hope infects the world
America's dream shines

White House opens door
a black man enters
America's sins redeemed
change makes the scene

Obama raises standard
charisma flows the land
people raise their heads
singing songs of hope

In the changing of the guard
a new generation takes hold
belligerence left behind
non-violence is on the rise

World's tide runs full
stormy seas await
energy and motion fill
the vacuum of our hearts

Where to Mr. Obama?

Rejoice and repeat
past is ever prologue

Forgive and forget
those who trespassed
the Constitution
the rule of law
the rights of man

Forgive and forget
the lies to war
the plundered treasury
the maimed and dead
the tragic American dilemma

Forgive and forget
the graft and corruption
the glut in corporate welfare
the righteousness to torture

Rejoice in the future
never look back
history never repeats
togetherness is all

We told the Nazis
pay for your sins
Obama tells the Bush-Cheneys
rejoice and retire
you did no wrong

Our government
it's just a game

Capitalism today

My world is grasping
in calligraphy of change
syn texted in dynamic rhythm
fax ricated in bytes of sound

Science and technology
create status to modern ego
raze frenzy to human endeavor
flame engines escalating desire

Gods of the market place
derive all value
subvert our ethics
dictate our government

People of our world
seek blessing in many religions
pay tribute to many gods
twirl into poverty

Ode to Super Bowl

American karma unfolds
in Super Bowl arena
franchise of American dream
destiny not far behind

Signals nation's power
quantity of brawn
quality of brain
blended to machine relevance

Fame and fortune acclaim
unending replay
talking heads chant
cadence in idiotic mantra

Multitudes worship
as gladiators thrust
body to body
shudder their brains

Beer and sex intermingle
beatitudes of Madison Avenue
global corps dance tunes
to consumer virtue

Half-time pageants
geared in sexual flavors
theater to opulence
irrelevant to mankind

Don't Mine My Future

Another day of infamy
December 7th 2009
Japanese Glacier Northwest
attacks Maury Island

Yesterday Oliver opened his FBI file
standing on wind-swept beach
bathed in shivering damp fog
Oliver marches with sundry crowd
carrying banner of protest

Japanese-owned world conglomerate
brought their crane to rural Maury
to scoop the sand
harvest the rock
mine the watershed
poison the aquifer
lay desolate land and sound

Like generations before him
Oliver now anoints FBI register
civil disobedience
noted in peaceful protest
long a family tradition

Poppa Jack cut his teeth
chanted anti-war cadence
against cold war ignition
marched for civil rights in '63
hit the bricks again Viet Nam

Father Derek felled by tear gas
protesting Clinton's WTO
pounded bricks about Iraq

Now generations march on

Glimpses on Reed
a lobotomistic adventure

Today I tune to times
in memories chasm
when my universe
birthed new reality

Oral history kindles
ancient stories
hidden in shadowy murk
cradled in campus cocoon

Re-entering Reed's caldron
energized anew
veterans shedding war
flying banners of peace
dreaming new worlds

Old friends new friends
powering professors
challenging demands
papers struggling
to light the day

Elliot Winch
    Library Commons
Woodstock Canyon
    and Annna Mann
sex and beer and bridge
capped in coffee shop
    discourse

Intellect discovered
Arragon, McKinley, Stuart,
Knowlton, Scott, and Griffin
scratched new furrows
filled fallow ground

Arragon strides
English tweeds flying
McKinley always draped
in bureaucratic cloth
Stuart suited
in Wall Street charts
Knowlton rolls balls
bowing balded head
Scott sprouts
brown tweeded atoms
Leigh's plaids highlight
Malthusian logic
Griffin's wrinkled suit
attracts clouds of chalk
Jones' furrows squint
in Richard II's style

Life's innocence peaked
iron curtain went up
Wallace and Truman
liberalism challenged

Hit the bricks
man the barricades
raise the banner
list with the F B and I

Mountains claimed my soul
snow painted beauty
skis sent me flying
looking for my future

Thesis is done
happy is the cow
college ends
hail
era of no return

Lobotomy works

a little postscript for our 60th

Tonight the table reflects
our visions of ourselves
when we walked our walk
talked our talk
in growing dimensions
of worlds we knew not then

IV. Hardship and Change

The last summer

It was that July day in 1938
I was 12
Art was 14
we were swimming
just beyond the waves

Letting go of brother Art
he sinking into ocean froth
I struggling for shore

Out of breath
out of time
waves washed me in
my body felt the sand

Art is gone I cried
Father running down the beach
he waded in, looking out
trying to find his son
beneath the sea

Art's gone I cried out
and so the summer died
for our family and me

And looking back
just a lot of me
went into the sea

That day our family dissolved
Mother cried til she died
Dad locked up tight
and threw away the key

Frozen

Jumbled up all around
are things not done
I could make quite a list
and feel even worse

But then there's strength
in what I have done

Growth inside makes me weary
old miseries were so comfy

New discipline is hard to follow
change comes even harder
when life's course is charted
from frozen rudders

The G N P and H 2 O

Water is an element called H 2 O
so elemental
we say it's free
certainly not part of our G N P

Water constitutes most of me
water runs through me
and all living things
but does not count in the G N P

Rivers are veins networking mother earth
creating and expending vast energies
carrying rain drops to ocean storage
no way a part of the G N P

When rivers were pristine
they were home to many beings
but housing for Nature's things
certainly not counted in our G N P

Only when we made public works
for levies and dams to control water wild
and harness its uses for economy
did rivers start counting in the G N P

Dumping wastes of human spoil
expanding uses for sewage toil
swallowing industry's raw materials
eating the O from the H 2 O

Rivers still don't count in the G N P
all fish rely on Nature's gifts of water
only aquatic fellows caught on hooks
get to be part of the G N P

You will find almost everywhere
that Nature's services to mankind
go unrecognized by economic minds
fooled by the myth of the G N P

So how pray tell can man measure
efficiencies of earth mother's rivers
and productivity per hour of river mile
when water can't get into the G N P?

Down and up with the knee

A day of renewal

Behind blue shroud
world casts shimmering lights
blares most worrisome sounds

Looking upward as to heaven
laid out ready for wake
fear pervades deep down

Bright metal reflects strange objects
threatening blue shadows surround
hostile murmurs hustle beyond

No feeling down there
nudged like a ferry docking
alas it has begun

Talking poetry and nonsense
to anesthesiologist
fears dampen down

The crew below
sounds right serious
as the sawing begins

Saws and hammers work away
discard body parts
insert technology

Mood changes
room relaxes
satisfaction grunts from below

Waiting continues
discomfort beckons
shroud comes down

Face enclosed in space mask
announces in brimming pride
one hour and twenty two minutes
and forty more to sew you up

That's it...NEXT?

Blue shroud revisited

Black uncertainty uncurls
as news of staph unveils
new knee colors angry

Emergency room beckons
grim surgeon interrupted
with news of job gone bad

Where did this come from
and how did it get in?
pointing at patient

Start the antibiotics
no need for a culture
back to hospital bed

Start again
this unscheduled repeat
a redo for the surgeon

Angry patient
angry surgeon
incompetent anesthesiologist

No need for patient records
no teamwork here
just get it done

Derek helps through the night
pain not controlled
nurses come and go
anger and pain prevail

Awakening

Black carnage rumbles
destitute in purgatory
unknown blankets
sunk in murky well

Struck by staph
encased in hospital bounds
captured by surgeon
I gave up me to them

Now what?

Back from purgatory
opportunity beckons
climb from murky well

Where to go
what to change
get well in body
straight in mind

Take charge of me
dedicate to walk
reduce the bulk
seek inner peace

Ask for what I want
face death head on
build relationships
return to meditation

And just sail on
day into day

30 years sober

Today I celebrate
free from bondage
dark as slavery
binding as iron

Alcohol was my prison
seductive in its origin
facilitator of elbow
multiplier of thirst

Born to broken gut
alcohol knew no rein
from teens to fifty
I swilled bottles dry

This disease starts in fun
releases tension
kindles the wit
lights party fire

Devolution engulfs
anger and self pity
bottle enshrouds
love of self prevails

Time marches
disease engages
relationships falter
darkness beckons

Where to I am
no where to go
then a meeting
I did find

Fellow travelers
rise out of purgatory
meet to talk
share our stories

90 days and 90 meetings
'I am an alcoholic'
let go let god

Bar friends drop
meeting goers surround
life begins anew
rosy dawns glimmer

Meeting after meeting
I reach for help
extend my arms
aid fellow drunks

We hear our stories
share our tears
know we're together
in search of sober life

Healing emphysema

Yesterday it was
black heaviness
pressing on the chest
longed for release exploded

Just all at once
black fear erupted
from storage vaults
carved in bodily niches

Years of holding cigarettes
between twitching lips
inhaling emotions
and nicotine deep
co-mingled in black fear

Thanks to healer's hands
and universal energy
breath comes normal now
love not afraid of fear

There's only me

I struggle down life's corridors
wandering from room to room
searching always searching
for deep down reality

I scoured the temples
of Christ, Buddha, et al
climbed Nature's peaks
drank beauty from earth's bounty

The opiates of our culture
often traveled as my companion
I have sought states of bliss
and caught jagged hangovers

I sit in dutiful meditation
breathe into yogi
contemplate mind and body
extrapolating into external fiction

I look unto other humans
and want to be like them
or dream of soaring into yonder
with wings of the Osprey

When I add it all up
the only reality
that the I of me can find
is that deep down awareness of me

Old boots

In the back of my closet
deck boots linger
gathered in dust
hovering in history

Black knee-deep sides
white docksider soles
rebelling in retirement
barnacled in age

As I cast them into recycling
eons of memories unreel

Wind whistles
shrouds chime
seas slosh
boots grip

Mark to windward
skipper shouts
coming up
jibs stretched home

Many a Sunday
we rounded marks
knocked down and then again
adrift in breathless sky

Up and down the Chesapeake
across to eastern shore
wind abeam or aft
we linger in god's world

From Annapolis to Newport
white water flying
rounded Hatteras
stretching ten knots
covered in foam

Some boots are made
     for walking
my boots are made for sailing
and now
cast adrift
     in yesterday's waters

Uphill revisited

Dark shadows grow longer
sun rises over North Mountain
paints sky brilliant
blue ridge mist glimmers
snow dusts far ridge

Uphill holler breathes
silent crunchy leaves
lonely woodpecker
lines of apple trees
naked forest canopies

Black and brown armies
march their shadows
as dusk gathers

On age and youth

Time sometimes makes things
more difficult

Youth seeks out the easy chair
gains it with a leap
throws a leg across the arm
sinks in cushions deep

Age seeks out the straight hard chair
perches like a cup
age must think when sitting down
of the getting up

V. Wisdom and Peace

Pumpkin Sunday
Rising moon
Loveword bound
Sadness down the lane
Kass
The four flurry
Together
Permission to come aboard sir?
Last train ride
Burst of color
Kayaking with Barry
Walking with Wendell
Dawn in paradise
Filial advice
Ten pesos
My shadow

Pumpkin Sunday

I am here
I am not there

Candle flame wandered
through skeins of orange and yellow
flickering low
flaming high

I felt and saw hands from both sides
waving and beckoning
then beckoning and waving

Love and sadness
tranquility and fear
flowed between us

Yurt ceiling played roulette
zoomed in
then out

Doors of change opened
I may have crossed over
but they wouldn't let me go

Love knew no bounds

Rising moon

I met a young woman
now old in body
spirits still aglow
hormonal fever emerging

Entrapped in salsa rhythm
we danced the dance
encircled in love's embrace
climbed heights of ecstasy

And now we encircle
in new dimensions
testing waters
both hot and cold

Let your dreams unfold
as inner child shines anew
through grownup clouds
gathered in years gone by

Sadness down the lane

As I turned the corner
starting down Cougar Lane
there was a sadness in the air
a loss felt quite deep

It is just not believable
Willard and Marianne
packing up and moving out
of Lucas family home

Long in friendship
knowing the two
in this place so full
of loving tradition

Coddling memories
mixed with tales tall
that abound and resound
all around our Agness commune

I know full well
the humor of the man
shucking his sweet corn
in dawn's cool sun

Harvesting melons so mellow
picking tomatoes with Agness lush
while Marianne and crew
set the chickens to the fry

A clothespin opens the gate
to trencherman's delight
table filled with ancient bowls
loaded with farm family fare

Of the lore of Lucas Ranch
there is a fly rod of my name
I always wonder how many fish
caught alas not in my hand

Humor implanted in the vintage
of the house and grounds
one feels amongst the rendition
of early pioneer tradition

On the porch out front
made for sitting and the spitting
one can find Larry's shade
sitting in corner chair

In the winter's solitude
Marianne on the tube
Willard dozing in his chair
cracking wit in my ear

As far as I could see
Willard runs this farm
with bailing wire technososo
and horse sense bravadoso

In our sadness in their leaving
we find joy in the knowing
they were here for so many
to share the family tradition

Kass

I penned a few lines to Kass the day she died
that went something like this…

They tell me you are going to hang it up

Beat me to the finish line are you?

Well if that's the case, fair thee well

I'll probably tag right behind
and catch you on the sunrise

I want to tell you Kass
you gathered the love of family and friends
and bundled our affections in mixes of emotions
like tough, ornery, thoughtful, loving, and kind

You made well your mark on this land

In 86 years of living
you lived the land and loved the rivers
felt the seasons change
stewarded well your inheritance
worked your hands deep in the soil
raised the garden
canned the harvest
and baked my chocolate pies

Grand dam on the road of Spud
a fierce competitor on Squaw's Bar
the springers are your lust

You hunted the hills
and filled the larder

We all thank you for being you
and sharing your life with us

Loveword bound

There she was
bent over
rear skyward
trimming heather
in the garden of Dhamma

A serious laughing face
a twinkle in her eye
I felt the magic swirling
and knew there was more

Now we are at sea
awash in worlds of being
joined in eternal fray
man and woman

How shall we set sail
into this destiny
we ask ourselves
and each other

Like two ships passing in the night
entwined in folds of black delight
let our bodies say it all
and stay our course come the dawn

The four flurry

It's hard to keep up with Oliver
he's a-speeding up
and I'm a-slowing down

He jumps to the world
in exponential claim
while Poppa pulls in reins
most functions in decline

When it comes to reading
he's always on the ready
hefting book climbing laps
while Poppa's in recline

Gleaning is his bent
no berry left behind
bugs birds and bees
harken his attention

Debuting on Gandhi's stage
protested mine with civil sign
stood tall agin library move
made hay in journalistic fray

So blow the candles
sing the song
stand aside
Oliver's on the move

Together

On Father's Day
I salute my son
parading
new father's banner

Down the landscape of years
we have glided
father and son
parsing life's corridors

Now in grandfatherly glow
I watch Derek and Oliver
join hands
as father and son

To take their walk
talk their talk
down life's path
into their life cycle

Let us celebrate
all things past and future
of love and life together

Permission to come aboard sir?

A half century to unwind
four score to celebrate

Like two kids in a pod
we've sailed bay and sound
up down and across
and back again

Hoisting sail after sail
desolate and gray
blue clouds scudding
steamy breath enshrouding

Dancing with whitecaps
challenging skipjacks
beating to windward
running by the lee

Round the buoys
up to starboard
Jack sets pole
spinnaker flashes

As tide runs free
Captain Allan
carries helm
across the line

We rinky dinks
still gather round
sopping beer
sailing again and again

Now in rocking chairs
we feather stories
clasp our friendship dear
tend to our dreams
and watch the setting sun

Last train ride

The day my friend Allan died
I had a dream that went like this

Death swings aboard the caboose
collecting tickets
on the last train ride

Walks quietly
through the cars
counting the miles

Cold breeze chills
heads turn as door opens
credit is foreclosed

Silent and patient
I hand up my ticket
on this last train ride

Burst of color

I have something to say to you
yes you...Merry Jakovics

About how you and I
creatures of the soil
talk to plants and flowers
who grace your yard
in brilliant display
winding through seasons

How on your corner
we politicians hang our signs
leaning out to shout our names
to numb the mind and train the hand
to mark the X for me

No English garden for you
it isn't in your eastern blood
masses of color
sound out your message

And I say thanks for the color
you flash to each of us
from your corner
through the garden of my life

Kayaking with Barry

Eyes penetrating and receiving
from smile twittering face
wrinkles beam in greeting
a wistful shrug says hello

We clasp in warmth
feel the moment now
in this time and place
as our friendship flows

Humor imbues your ethos
slightly hunched
you live this world
with earnest hope

Barry you sit upstream
keeping eye on Illinois things
hear our river sing and sigh
as you ponder down its currents

Paddle dipping in rhythmic tone
I see you slip downriver
gliding through historic time
enjoying the riparian moment

In the battle for conservation
you made a lot of marks
with heart, soul, and work
in Siskiyou Project doings

My friend I love and cherish you
let's walk our walk
and keep talking our talk

Walking with Wendell

Sing the song of Nature's wonder
dance with fairies in sun speckled forest
pay tribute for our walks with Wendell
as he shared his knowledge of place and flora

Wendell answered a deep call from the wild
as he walked his trail
defending Nature's integrity

Up and down our state
from Klamath to the coast
his praises forever flow

Projecting deep knowledge
his trail tutorials live on
spun in kindness and humor

Yes in the history of conservation
Wendell dwells well
with Thoreau, Marshall, and Muir

And we thank him for making our trail
so much more exciting

Dawn in paradise

Night black fades
grays come alive
shadows sweep far hills
pink frames new day

Sun and shadow
begin their dance
cross land sea and sky

I walk my beach
birds begin their work
waves flat
sea lazy

My soul generates
a calmness in the moment

Filial advice

Wonder on
while life grants you freedom
to roam the world
to feel the mundane

Wonder on
while youth quest
still burns bright
in body and soul

Wander on
to hear the night winds
bellow across the steppes
holler up the canyons

Wander on
to feel bus lurch and lunge
over rocky road
groaning up and up

Wander on
til your heart tells you
this quest is over
I am ready for the next

ten pesos sit
two raindrops glitter
sun creeps day follows

My shadow never leaves
walking north shadow trails
walking south shadow leads
I and my shadow are one

About the Author

Jack Churchill, born in 1926, adopted the mantle of poet late in life, after serving as an agent of change in national and local environmental policies for over five decades.

Jack's early years were spent in Portland, Oregon, with summers at Neahkannie Beach. After service in the U.S. Army and graduation from Reed College and Harvard School of Government, he moved to Washington, D.C., to begin his career as a political economist. Jack worked on new policies for stewarding our nation's public lands and waters. He served in the Secretary's office of the Department of Agriculture and Interior's Bureau of Land Management. Jack also helped form the Environmental Protection Agency and shape the Clean Water Act.

After the environmental decade of the 70s, Jack moved home to help implement Oregon's Clean Water Act and begin teaching as Adjunct Professor of Water and Land Policy at Portland State University. He served on the Lake Oswego City Council and as an advisor to the State Legislature. He was a citizen activist in many judicial and regulatory controversies concerning the environment.

His poetry flows from these experiences and life in his wilderness home along the waters of the Tom Fry.

Jack now divides his time between Vashon Island, Washington, and his tree farm at the confluence of the Illinois and Rogue Rivers near Agness, Oregon.